VEG
COOKBO
ATHLETES

Dessert and Snack

—

Sauces and Dips

+51 High-Protein Delicious Recipes for a Plant-Based Diet Plan and For a Strong Body While Maintaining Health, Vitality and Energy

—
3

Description

As an athlete, it may sound like the vegan diet may not provide you the right Nutrition. But I am sure after reading these recipes; you can very well debunk that myth.

Inside this guide, there is a bunch of tasty and easy to cook recipes which will make sure that you get your share of protein and carbs. Remember that while being a meat free athlete ain't easy, this is hardly a reason to quit!

One of the greatest benefits of going vegan is the increased level of health you will experience and this manifests well beyond just your physique. Add to this the potent combination of healthy plant-based protein and you have a winner! You can also choose to supplement with vegan protein powder.

Remember to prep your meals ahead of time for maximum convenience. This guide covers the following recipes:

- Breakfast
- Lunch
- Dessert
- Desserts and snacks
- Sauces and dips

Happy Cooking!!

INTRODUCTION TO THE VEGAN DIET

A lot of people seeking to avoid a lifestyle that contributes to disorders and diseases such as heart attacks, type II diabetes and even cancer go Vegan. These people usually go vegan in order to reduce the intake of animal products and the harmful effects they can have on the body.

Most vegan products are plant based and they reduce the risk of these terrible diseases as well as lowering the risk of developing Alzheimer's disease and many others.

A Vegan diet also contributes to weight loss, not only is a plant-based diet less calorie dense, but provides the right nutrients to slim down quickly. A Vegan diet lowers cholesterol levels, LDLs and blood pressure - this will make you not only feel great, but look great too. In fact, people on a vegan diet typically have their blood pressure 25-75% lower than a person with an animal product diet. This also puts Vegans at a far lower risk of dementia.

Essentially, a Vegan diet will create a healthy lifestyle without even needing to work out. If you do work out as well though, that can produce some incredible results in terms of both weight loss and health! I will explore some of these benefits further later on in the book.

In addition, a lot of the antibiotics used in the modern animal farming system cause a lot of terrible side effects, and by going Vegan people are avoiding these.

For example, excess oestrogen, which is used in order to make animals more 'plump' to increase the meat industries 'yield', can contribute to weight gain when consumed by humans. In addition, high levels of oestrogen have been linked to gynecomastia (colloqually referred to as 'man boobs') in men.

DESSERT AND SNACK RECIPES

Banana-Nut Bread Bars

Preparation time: 5 minutes
Cooking time: 30 minutes
Servings: 9 bars

Ingredients
Nonstick cooking spray (optional)
2 large ripe bananas
1 tablespoon maple syrup
½ Teaspoon vanilla extract
2 cups old-fashioned rolled oats
½ Teaspoons salt
¼ Cup chopped walnuts

Directions:
Preheat the oven to 350°f. Lightly coat a 9-by-9-inch baking pan with nonstick cooking spray (if using) or line with parchment paper for oil-free baking.
In a medium bowl, mash the bananas with a fork. Add the maple syrup and vanilla extract and mix well. Add the oats, salt, and walnuts, mixing well.
Transfer the batter to the baking pan and bake for 25 to 30 minutes, until the top is crispy. Cool completely before slicing into 9 bars. Transfer to an airtight storage container or a large plastic bag.
Nutrition (1 bar): calories: 73; fat: 1g; protein: 2g; carbohydrates: 15g; fiber: 2g; sugar: 5g; sodium: 129mg

Lemon Coconut Cilantro Rolls

Preparation time: 30 minutes • chill time: 30 minutes
Servings: 16 pieces
Ingredients

½ Cup fresh cilantro, chopped
1 cup sprouts (clover, alfalfa)
1 garlic clove, pressed
2 tablespoons ground brazil nuts or almonds
2 tablespoons flaked coconut
1 tablespoon coconut oil
Pinch cayenne pepper
Pinch sea salt
Pinch freshly ground black pepper
Zest and juice of 1 lemon
2 tablespoons ground flaxseed
1 to 2 tablespoons water
2 whole-wheat wraps, or corn wraps

Directions:
Put everything but the wraps in a food processor and pulse to combine. Or combine the Ingredients in a large bowl. Add the water, if needed, to help the mix come together.
Spread the mixture out over each wrap, roll it up, and place it in the fridge for 30 minutes to set.
Remove the rolls from the fridge and slice each into 8 pieces to serve as appetizers or sides with a soup or stew.
Get the best flavor by buying whole raw brazil nuts or almonds, toasting them lightly in a dry skillet or toaster oven, and then grinding them in a coffee grinder.
Nutrition (1 piece) calories: 66; total fat: 4g; carbs: 6g; fiber: 1g; protein: 2g

Tamari Almonds

Preparation time: 5 minutes
Cooking time: 15 minutes
Servings: 8
Ingredients

1 pound raw almonds
3 tablespoons tamari or soy sauce
2 tablespoons extra-virgin olive oil
1 tablespoon Nutritional yeast
1 to 2 teaspoons chili powder, to taste

Directions:
Preheat the oven to 400°f.
Line a baking sheet with parchment paper.
In a medium bowl, combine the almonds, tamari, and olive oil until well coated.
Spread the almonds on the prepared baking sheet and roast for 10 to 15 minutes, until browned.
Cool for 10 minutes, then season with the Nutritional yeast and chili powder.
Transfer to a glass jar and close tightly with a lid.
Nutrition: calories: 364; fat: 32g; protein: 13g; carbohydrates: 13g; fiber: 7g; sugar: 3g; sodium: 381mg

Tempeh Taco Bites

Preparation time: 5 minutes
Cooking time: 45 minutes
Servings: 3 dozen
Ingredients

8 ounces tempeh
3 tablespoons soy sauce
2 teaspoons ground cumin
1 teaspoon chili powder
1 teaspoon dried oregano
1 tablespoon olive oil
1⁄2 cup finely minced onion
2 garlic cloves, minced
Salt and freshly ground black pepper
2 tablespoons tomato paste
1 chipotle chile in adobo, finely minced
1⁄4 cup hot water or vegetable broth, homemade or store-bought, plus more if needed
36 phyllo pastry cups, thawed
1⁄2 cup basic guacamole, homemade or store-bought
18 ripe cherry tomatoes, halved

Directions

In a medium saucepan of simmering water, cook the tempeh for 30 minutes. Drain well, then finely mince and place it in a bowl. Add the soy sauce, cumin, chili powder, and oregano. Mix well and set aside.

In a medium skillet, heat the oil over medium heat. Add the onion, cover, and cook for 5 minutes. Stir in the garlic, then add the tempeh mixture and cook, stirring, for 2 to 3 minutes. Season with salt and pepper to taste. Set aside.

In a small bowl, combine the tomato paste, chipotle, and the hot water or broth. Return tempeh mixture to heat and in stir tomato-chile mixture and cook for 10 to 15 minutes, stirring occasionally, until the liquid is absorbed.

The mixture should be fairly dry, but if it begins to stick to the pan, add a little more hot water, 1 tablespoon at a time. Taste, adjusting seasonings if necessary. Remove from the heat.
To assemble, fill the phyllo cups to the top with the tempeh filling, using about 2 teaspoons of filling in each. Top with a dollop of guacamole and a cherry tomato half and serve.

Mushroom Croustades

Preparation time: 10 minutes
Cooking time: 10 minutes
Servings: 12 croustades
Ingredients

12 thin slices whole-grain bread
1 tablespoon olive oil, plus more for brushing bread
2 medium shallots, chopped
2 garlic cloves, minced
12 ounces white mushrooms, chopped
1/4 cup chopped fresh parsley
1 teaspoon dried thyme
1 tablespoon soy sauce

Directions

Preheat the oven to 400°f. Using a 3-inch round pastry cutter or a drinking glass, cut a circle from each bread slice. Brush the bread circles with oil and press them firmly but gently into a mini-muffin tin. Bake until the bread is toasted, about 10 minutes.
Meanwhile, in a large skillet, heat the 1 tablespoon oil over medium heat. Add the shallots, garlic, and mushrooms and sauté for 5 minutes to soften the vegetables. Stir in the parsley, thyme, and soy sauce and cook until the liquid is absorbed, about 5 minutes longer. Spoon the mushroom mixture into the croustade cups and return to the oven for 3 to 5 minutes to heat through. Serve warm.

Stuffed Cherry Tomatoes

Preparation time: 15 minutes
Cooking time: 0 minutes
Servings: 6
Ingredients

2 pints cherry tomatoes, tops removed and centers scooped out
2 avocados, mashed
Juice of 1 lemon
½ Red bell pepper, minced
4 green onions (white and green parts), finely minced
1 tablespoon minced fresh tarragon
Pinch of sea salt

Directions:
Place the cherry tomatoes open-side up on a platter.
In a small bowl, -combine the avocado, lemon juice, bell pepper,
scallions, tarragon, and salt.
Stir until well -combined. Scoop into the cherry tomatoes and serve
immediately.

Spicy Black Bean Dip

Preparation time: 10 minutes
Cooking time: 0 minutes
Servings: 2 cups
Ingredients
1 (14-ounce) can black beans, drained and rinsed, or 1½ cups cooked
Zest and juice of 1 lime
1 tablespoon tamari, or soy sauce
¼ Cup water
¼ Cup fresh cilantro, chopped
1 teaspoon ground cumin
Pinch cayenne pepper

Directions:
Put the beans in a food processor (best choice) or blender, along with the lime zest and juice, tamari, and about ¼ cup of water. Blend until smooth, then blend in the cilantro, cumin, and cayenne.
If you don't have a blender or prefer a different consistency, simply transfer it to a bowl once the beans have been puréed and stir in the spices, instead of forcing the blender.
Nutrition (1 cup) calories: 190; total fat: 1g; carbs: 35g; fiber: 12g; protein: 13g

French Onion Pastry Puffs

Preparation time: 10 minutes
Cooking time: 35 minutes - makes 24 puffs
Ingredients

2 tablespoons olive oil
2 medium sweet yellow onions, thinly sliced
1 garlic clove, minced
1 teaspoon chopped fresh rosemary
Salt and freshly ground black pepper
1 tablespoon capers
1 sheet frozen vegan puff pastry, thawed
18 pitted black olives, quartered

Directions
In a medium skillet, heat the oil over medium heat. Add the onions
and garlic, season with rosemary and salt and pepper to taste. Cover
and cook until very soft, stirring occasionally, about 20 minutes. Stir
in the capers and set aside.
Preheat the oven to 400°f. Roll out the puff pastry and cut into 2- to
3-inch circles using a lightly floured pastry cutter or drinking glass.
You should get about 2 dozen circles.
Arrange the pastry circles on baking sheets and top each with a
heaping teaspoon of onion mixture, patting down to smooth the top.
Top with 3 olive quarters, arranged decoratively—either like flower
petals emanating from the center or parallel to each other like 3
bars.
Bake until pastry is puffed and golden brown, about 15 minutes.
Serve hot.

Cheezy Cashew–Roasted Red Pepper Toasts

Preparation time: 15 minutes
Cooking time: 0 minutes
Servings: 16 to 24 toasts
Ingredients

2 jarred roasted red peppers
1 cup unsalted cashews
1/4 cup water
1 tablespoon soy sauce
2 tablespoons chopped green onions
1/4 cup Nutritional yeast
2 tablespoons balsamic vinegar
2 tablespoons olive oil

Directions
Use canapé or cookie cutters to cut the bread into desired shapes about 2 inches wide. If you don't have a cutter, use a knife to cut the bread into squares, triangles, or rectangles. You should get 2 to 4 pieces out of each slice of bread. Toast the bread and set aside to cool.
Coarsely chop 1 red pepper and set aside. Cut the remaining pepper into thin strips or decorative shapes and set aside for garnish.
In a blender or food processor, grind the cashews to a fine powder. Add the water and soy sauce and process until smooth. Add the chopped red pepper and puree. Add the green onions, Nutritional yeast, vinegar, and oil and process until smooth and well blended.

Spread a spoonful of the pepper mixture onto each of the toasted bread pieces and top decoratively with the reserved pepper strips. Arrange on a platter or tray and serve.

Baked Potato Chips

Preparation time: 10 minutes
Cooking time: 30 minutes
Servings: 4
Ingredients

1 large russet potato
1 teaspoon paprika
½ Teaspoon garlic salt
¼ Teaspoon vegan sugar
¼ Teaspoon onion powder
¼ Teaspoon chipotle powder or chili powder
⅛ Teaspoon salt
⅛ Teaspoon ground mustard
⅛ Teaspoon ground cayenne pepper
1 teaspoon canola oil
⅛ Teaspoon liquid smoke

Directions:
Wash and peel the potato. Cut into thin, 1/10-inch slices (a mandoline slicer or the slicer blade in a food processor is helpful for consistently sized slices).
Fill a large bowl with enough very cold water to cover the potato. Transfer the potato slices to the bowl and soak for 20 minutes.
Preheat the oven to 400°f. Line a baking sheet with parchment paper.
In a small bowl, combine the paprika, garlic salt, sugar, onion powder, chipotle powder, salt, mustard, and cayenne.
Drain and rinse the potato slices and pat dry with a paper towel.

Transfer to a large bowl.

Add the canola oil, liquid smoke, and spice mixture to the bowl. Toss to coat.

Transfer the potatoes to the prepared baking sheet.

Bake for 15 minutes. Flip the chips over and bake for 15 minutes longer, until browned. Transfer the chips to 4 storage containers or large glass jars.

Let cool before closing the lids tightly.

Nutrition: calories: 89; fat: 1g; protein: 2g; carbohydrates: 18g; fiber: 2g; sugar: 1g; sodium: 65mg

Mushrooms Stuffed With Spinach And Walnuts

Preparation time: 10 minutes
Cooking time: 6 minutes
Servings: 4 to 6 servings
Ingredients

2 tablespoons olive oil
8 ounces white mushroom, lightly rinsed, patted dry, and stems reserved
1 garlic clove, minced
1 cup cooked spinach
1 cup finely chopped walnuts
1/2 cup unseasoned dry bread crumbs
Salt and freshly ground black pepper

Directions
Preheat the oven to 400°f. Lightly oil a large baking pan and set aside. In a large skillet, heat the oil over medium heat. Add the mushroom caps and cook for 2 minutes to soften slightly. Remove from the skillet and set aside.
Chop the mushroom stems and add to the same skillet. Add the garlic and cook over medium heat until softened, about 2 minutes. Stir in the spinach, walnuts, bread crumbs, and salt and pepper to taste. Cook for 2 minutes, stirring well to combine.
Fill the reserved mushroom caps with the stuffing mixture and arrange in the baking pan. Bake until the mushrooms are tender and the filling is hot, about 10 minutes. Serve hot.

Salsa Fresca

Preparation time: 15 minutes
Cooking time: 0 minutes
Servings: 4
Ingredients

3 large heirloom tomatoes or other fresh tomatoes, chopped
½ Red onion, finely chopped
½ Bunch cilantro, chopped
2 garlic cloves, minced
1 jalapeño, minced
Juice of 1 lime, or 1 tablespoon prepared lime juice
¼ Cup olive oil
Sea salt
Whole-grain tortilla chips, for serving

Directions:
In a small bowl, combine the tomatoes, onion, cilantro, garlic, jalapeño, lime juice, and olive oil and mix well. Allow to sit at room temperature for 15 minutes. Season with salt.
Serve with tortilla chips.
The salsa can be stored in an airtight container in the refrigerator for up to 1 week.

Guacamole

Preparation time: 10 minutes
Cooking time: 0 minutes
Servings: 2
Ingredients

2 ripe avocados
2 garlic cloves, pressed
Zest and juice of 1 lime
1 teaspoon ground cumin
Pinch sea salt
Pinch freshly ground black pepper
Pinch cayenne pepper (optional)

Directions:
Mash the avocados in a large bowl. Add the rest of the Ingredients and stir to combine.
Try adding diced tomatoes (cherry are divine), chopped scallions or chives, chopped fresh cilantro or basil, lemon rather than lime, paprika, or whatever you think would taste good!
Nutrition (1 cup) calories: 258; total fat: 22g; carbs: 18g; fiber: 11g; protein: 4g

Veggie Hummus Pinwheels

Preparation time: 10 minutes
Cooking time: 0 minutes
Servings: 3
Ingredients

3 whole-grain, spinach, flour, or gluten-free tortillas
3 large swiss chard leaves
¾ Cup edamame hummus or prepared hummus
¾ Cup shredded carrots

Directions:
Lay 1 tortilla flat on a cutting board.
Place 1 swiss chard leaf over the tortilla. Spread ¼ cup of hummus over the swiss chard. Spread ¼ cup of carrots over the hummus. Starting at one end of the tortilla, roll tightly toward the opposite side.
Slice each roll up into 6 pieces. Place in a single-serving storage container.
Repeat with the remaining tortillas and filling and seal the lids.
Nutrition: calories: 254; fat: 8g; protein: 10g; carbohydrates: 39g; fiber: 8g; sugar: 4g; sodium: 488mg

Asian Lettuce Rolls

Preparation time: 15 minutes
Cooking time: 5 minutes
Servings: 4
Ingredients

2 ounces rice noodles
2 tablespoons chopped thai basil
2 tablespoons chopped cilantro
1 garlic clove, minced
1 tablespoon minced fresh ginger
Juice of ½ lime, or 2 teaspoons prepared lime juice
2 tablespoons soy sauce
1 cucumber, julienned
2 carrots, peeled and julienned
8 leaves butter lettuce

Directions:
Cook the rice noodles according to package Directions.
In a small bowl, whisk together the basil, cilantro, garlic, ginger, lime juice, and soy sauce. Toss with the cooked noodles, cucumber, and carrots.
Divide the mixture evenly among lettuce leaves and roll.
Secure with a toothpick and serve immediately.

Pinto-Pecan Fireballs

Preparation time: 5 minutes
Cooking time: 30 minutes
Servings: about 20 pieces
Ingredients

1-1⁄2 cups cooked or 1 (15.5-ounce) can pinto beans, drained and rinsed
1⁄2 cup chopped pecans
1⁄4 cup minced green onions
1 garlic clove, minced
3 tablespoons wheat gluten flour (vital wheat gluten)
3 tablespoons unseasoned dry bread crumbs
4 tablespoons tabasco or other hot sauce
1⁄4 teaspoon salt
1⁄8 teaspoon ground cayenne
1⁄4 cup vegan margarine

Directions
Preheat the oven to 350°f. Lightly oil a 9 x 13-inch baking pan and set aside. Blot the drained beans well with a paper towel, pressing out any excess liquid. In a food processor, combine the pinto beans, pecans, green onions, garlic, flour, bread crumbs, 2 tablespoons of the tabasco, salt, and cayenne. Pulse until well combined, leaving some texture. Use your hands to roll the mixture firmly into 1-inch balls.
Place the balls in the prepared baking pan and bake until nicely browned, about 25 to 30 minutes, turning halfway through.

Meanwhile, in small saucepan, combine the remaining 2 tablespoons tabasco and the margarine and melt over low heat. Pour the sauce over the fireballs and bake 10 minutes longer. Serve immediately.

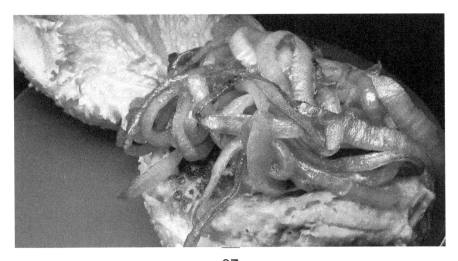

Sweet Potato Biscuits

Preparation time: 60 minutes
Cooking time: 10 minutes
Servings: 12 biscuits
Ingredients
1 medium sweet potato
3 tablespoons melted coconut oil, divided
1 tablespoon maple syrup
1 cup whole-wheat flour
2 teaspoons baking powder
Pinch sea salt
Directions:

Bake the sweet potato at 350°F for about 45 minutes, until tender.

Allow it to cool, then remove the flesh and mash.

Turn the oven up to 375°F and line a baking sheet with parchment paper or lightly grease it. Measure out 1 cup potato flesh.

In a medium bowl, combine the mashed sweet potato with 1½ tablespoons of the coconut oil and the maple syrup. Mix together the flour and baking powder in a separate medium bowl, then add the flour mixture to the potato mixture and blend well with a fork.

On a floured board, pat the mixture out into a ½-inch-thick circle and cut out 1-inch rounds, or simply drop spoonfuls of dough and pat them into rounds.

Put the rounds onto the prepared baking sheet. Brush the top of each with some of the remaining 1½ tablespoons melted coconut oil. Bake 10 minutes, or until lightly golden on top. Serve hot.

Nutrition (1 biscuit) calories: 116; total fat: 4g; carbs: 19g; fiber: 3g; protein: 3g

Lemon And Garlic Marinated Mushrooms

Preparation time: 15 minutes
Cooking time: 0 minutes
Servings: 4 servings
Ingredients

3 tablespoons olive oil
2 tablespoons fresh lemon juice
2 garlic cloves, crushed
1 teaspoon dried marjoram
1/2 teaspoon coarsely ground fennel seed
1/2 teaspoon salt
1/4 teaspoon freshly ground black pepper
8 ounces small white mushrooms, lightly rinsed, patted dry, and stemmed
1 tablespoon minced fresh parsley

Directions
In a medium bowl, whisk together the oil, lemon juice, garlic, marjoram, fennel seed, salt, and pepper. Add the mushrooms and parsley and stir gently until coated.
Cover and refrigerate for at least 2 hours or overnight. Stir well before serving.

Garlic Toast

Preparation time: 5 minutes
Cooking time: 5 minutes
Servings: 1 slice
Ingredients

1 teaspoon coconut oil, or olive oil
Pinch sea salt
1 to 2 teaspoons Nutritional yeast
1 small garlic clove, pressed, or ¼ teaspoon garlic powder
1 slice whole-grain bread

Directions:
In a small bowl, mix together the oil, salt, Nutritional yeast, and garlic.
You can either toast the bread and then spread it with the seasoned oil, or brush the oil on the bread and put it in a toaster oven to bake for 5 minutes.
If you're using fresh garlic, it's best to spread it onto the bread and then bake it.
Nutrition (1 slice) calories: 138; total fat: 6g; carbs: 16g; fiber: 4g; protein: 7g

Vietnamese-Style Lettuce Rolls

Preparation time: 15 minutes
Cooking time: 0 minutes
Servings: 4 servings
Ingredients

2 green onions
2 tablespoons soy sauce
2 tablespoons rice vinegar
1 teaspoon sugar
1/8 teaspoon crushed red pepper
3 tablespoons water
3 ounces rice vermicelli
4 to 6 soft green leaf lettuce leaves
1 medium carrot, shredded
1/2 medium english cucumber, peeled, seeded, and cut lengthwise into 1/4-inch strips
1/2 medium red bell pepper, cut into 1/4-inch strips
1 cup loosely packed fresh cilantro or basil leaves

Directions
Cut the green part off the green onions and cut them lengthwise into thin slices and set aside. Mince the white part of the green onions and transfer to a small bowl. Add the soy sauce, rice vinegar, sugar, crushed red pepper, and water. Stir to blend and set aside.

Soak the vermicelli in medium bowl of hot water until softened, about 1 minute. Drain the noodles well and cut them into 3-inch lengths. Set aside.
Place a lettuce leaf on a work surface and arrange a row of noodles in the center of the leaf, followed by a few strips of scallion greens, carrot, cucumber, bell pepper, and cilantro. Bring the bottom edge of the leaf over the filling and fold in the two short sides. Roll up gently but tightly. Place the roll seam side down on a serving platter. Repeat with
Remaining Ingredients. Serve with the dipping sauce.

Apple Crumble

Preparation time: 20 minutes
Cooking time: 25 minutes
Servings: 6
Ingredients

FOR THE FILLING
4 to 5 apples, cored and chopped (about 6 cups)
½ Cup unsweetened applesauce, or ¼ cup water
2 to 3 tablespoons unrefined sugar (coconut, date, sucanat, maple syrup)
1 teaspoon ground cinnamon
Pinch sea salt

FOR THE CRUMBLE
2 tablespoons almond butter, or cashew or sunflower seed butter
2 tablespoons maple syrup
1½ cups rolled oats
½ Cup walnuts, finely chopped
½ Teaspoon ground cinnamon
2 to 3 tablespoons unrefined granular sugar (coconut, date, sucanat)

Directions:
Preheat the oven to 350°f. Put the apples and applesauce in an 8-inch-square baking dish, and sprinkle with the sugar, cinnamon, and salt. Toss to combine.
In a medium bowl, mix together the nut butter and maple syrup until smooth and creamy. Add the oats, walnuts, cinnamon, and sugar and stir to coat, using your hands if necessary. (if you have a small food processor, pulse the oats and walnuts together before adding them to the mix.)
Sprinkle the topping over the apples, and put the dish in the oven.

———

Bake for 20 to 25 minutes, or until the fruit is soft and the topping is lightly browned.
Nutrition calories: 356; total fat: 17g; carbs: 49g; fiber: 7g; protein: 7g

Cashew-Chocolate Truffles

Preparation time: 15 minutes
Cooking time: 0 minutes • plus 1 hour to set
Servings: 12 truffles
Ingredients
1 cup raw cashews, soaked in water overnight
¾ Cup pitted dates
2 tablespoons coconut oil
1 cup unsweetened shredded coconut, divided
1 to 2 tablespoons cocoa powder, to taste
Directions:
In a food processor, combine the cashews, dates, coconut oil, ½ cup of shredded coconut, and cocoa powder. Pulse until fully incorporated; it will resemble chunky cookie dough. Spread the remaining ½ cup of shredded coconut on a plate.
Form the mixture into tablespoon-size balls and roll on the plate to cover with the shredded coconut. Transfer to a parchment paper–lined plate or baking sheet. Repeat to make 12 truffles.
Place the truffles in the refrigerator for 1 hour to set. Transfer the truffles to a storage container or freezer-safe bag and seal.
Nutrition (1 truffle): calories 238: fat: 18g; protein: 3g; carbohydrates: 16g; fiber: 4g; sugar: 9g; sodium: 9mg

Banana Chocolate Cupcakes

Preparation time: 20 minutes
Cooking time: 20 minutes
Servings: 12 cupcakes
Ingredients
3 medium bananas
1 cup non-dairy milk
2 tablespoons almond butter
1 teaspoon apple cider vinegar
1 teaspoon pure vanilla extract
1¼ cups whole-grain flour
½ Cup rolled oats
¼ Cup coconut sugar (optional)
1 teaspoon baking powder
½ Teaspoon baking soda
½ Cup unsweetened cocoa powder
¼ Cup chia seeds, or sesame seeds
Pinch sea salt
¼ Cup dark chocolate chips, dried cranberries, or raisins (optional)
Directions:
Preheat the oven to 350°f. Lightly grease the cups of two 6-cup
muffin tins or line with paper muffin cups.
Put the bananas, milk, almond butter, vinegar, and vanilla in a
blender and purée until smooth. Or stir together in a large bowl
until smooth and creamy.
Put the flour, oats, sugar (if using), baking powder, baking soda,
cocoa powder, chia seeds, salt, and chocolate chips in another large
bowl, and stir to combine. Mix together the wet and dry Ingredients,
stirring as little as possible. Spoon into muffin cups, and bake for 20
to 25 minutes. Take the cupcakes out of the oven and let them cool
fully before taking out of the muffin tins, since they'll be very moist.
Nutrition (1 cupcake) calories: 215; total fat: 6g; carbs: 39g; fiber:
9g; protein: 6g

Minty Fruit Salad

Preparation time: 15 minutes
Cooking time: 5 minutes
Servings: 4
Ingredients
¼ Cup lemon juice (about 2 small lemons)
4 teaspoons maple syrup or agave syrup
2 cups chopped pineapple
2 cups chopped strawberries
2 cups raspberries
1 cup blueberries
8 fresh mint leaves
Directions:
Beginning with 1 mason jar, add the Ingredients in this order:
1 tablespoon of lemon juice, 1 teaspoon of maple syrup, ½ cup of pineapple, ½ cup of strawberries, ½ cup of raspberries, ¼ cup of blueberries, and 2 mint leaves.
Repeat to fill 3 more jars. Close the jars tightly with lids.
Place the airtight jars in the refrigerator for up to 3 days.
Nutrition: calories: 138; fat: 1g; protein: 2g; carbohydrates: 34g; fiber: 8g; sugar: 22g; sodium: 6mg

Mango Coconut Cream Pie

Preparation time: 20 minutes • chill time: 30 minutes
Servings: 8
Ingredients

FOR THE CRUST
½ Cup rolled oats
1 cup cashews
1 cup soft pitted dates

FOR THE FILLING
1 cup canned coconut milk
½ Cup water
2 large mangos, peeled and chopped, or about 2 cups frozen chunks
½ Cup unsweetened shredded coconut

Directions:
Put all the crust Ingredients in a food processor and pulse until it holds together. If you don't have a food processor, chop everything as finely as possible and use ½ cup cashew or almond butter in place of half the cashews. Press the mixture down firmly into an 8-inch pie or springform pan.

Put the all filling Ingredients in a blender and purée until smooth (about 1 minute). It should be very thick, so you may have to stop and stir until it's smooth.

Pour the filling into the crust, use a rubber spatula to smooth the top, and put the pie in the freezer until set, about 30 minutes. Once frozen, it should be set out for about 15 minutes to soften before serving.

Top with a batch of coconut whipped cream scooped on top of the pie once it's set. Finish it off with a sprinkling of toasted shredded coconut.

Nutrition (1 slice) calories: 427; total fat: 28g; carbs: 45g; fiber: 6g; protein: 8g

Cherry-Vanilla Rice Pudding (pressure cooker)

Preparation time: 5 minutes
Serves 4-6
Ingredients
1 cup short-grain brown rice
1¾ cups nondairy milk, plus more as needed
1½ cups water
4 tablespoons unrefined sugar or pure maple syrup (use 2 tablespoons if you use a sweetened milk), plus more as needed
1 teaspoon vanilla extract (use ½ teaspoon if you use vanilla milk)
Pinch salt
¼ Cup dried cherries *or* ½ cup fresh or frozen pitted cherries
Directions
In your electric pressure cooker's cooking pot, combine the rice, milk, water, sugar, vanilla, and salt.
High pressure for 30 minutes. Close and lock the lid, and select high pressure for 30 minutes.
Pressure release. Once the cook time is complete, let the pressure release naturally, about 20 minutes. Unlock and remove the lid. Stir in the cherries and put the lid back on loosely for about 10 minutes. Serve, adding more milk or sugar, as desired.
Nutrition calories: 177; total fat: 1g; protein: 3g; sodium: 27mg; fiber: 2g

Mint Chocolate Chip Sorbet

Preparation time: 5 minutes
Cooking time: 0 minutes
Servings: 1
Ingredients
1 frozen banana
1 tablespoon almond butter, or peanut butter, or other nut or seed butter
2 tablespoons fresh mint, minced
¼ Cup or less non-dairy milk (only if needed)
2 to 3 tablespoons non-dairy chocolate chips, or cocoa nibs
2 to 3 tablespoons goji berries (optional)

Directions:
Put the banana, almond butter, and mint in a food processor or blender and purée until smooth.
Add the non-dairy milk if needed to keep blending (but only if needed, as this will make the texture less solid). Pulse the chocolate chips and goji berries (if using) into the mix so they're roughly chopped up.
Nutrition calories: 212; total fat: 10g; carbs: 31g; fiber: 4g; protein: 3g

Peach-Mango Crumble (pressure cooker)

Preparation time: 10 minutes
Serves 4-6
Ingredients
3 cups chopped fresh or frozen peaches
3 cups chopped fresh or frozen mangos
4 tablespoons unrefined sugar or pure maple syrup, divided
1 cup gluten-free rolled oats
½ Cup shredded coconut, sweetened or unsweetened
2 tablespoons coconut oil or vegan margarine
Directions
In a 6- to 7-inch round baking dish, toss together the peaches, mangos, and 2 tablespoons of sugar. In a food processor, combine the oats, coconut, coconut oil, and remaining 2 tablespoons of sugar. Pulse until combined. (if you use maple syrup, you'll need less coconut oil. Start with just the syrup and add oil if the mixture isn't sticking together.) Sprinkle the oat mixture over the fruit mixture. Cover the dish with aluminum foil. Put a trivet in the bottom of your electric pressure cooker's cooking pot and pour in a cup or two of water. Using a foil sling or silicone helper handles, lower the pan onto the trivet.
High pressure for 6 minutes. Close and lock the lid, and select high pressure for 6 minutes.
Pressure release. Once the cook time is complete, quick release the pressure. Unlock and remove the lid.
Let cool for a few minutes before carefully lifting out the dish with oven mitts or tongs. Scoop out portions to serve.
Nutrition calories: 321; total fat: 18g; protein: 4g; sodium: 2mg; fiber: 7g

Zesty Orange-Cranberry Energy Bites

Preparation time: 10 minutes • chill time: 15 minutes
Servings: 12 bites
Ingredients
2 tablespoons almond butter, or cashew or sunflower seed butter
2 tablespoons maple syrup, or brown rice syrup
¾ Cup cooked quinoa
¼ Cup sesame seeds, toasted
1 tablespoon chia seeds
½ Teaspoon almond extract, or vanilla extract
Zest of 1 orange
1 tablespoon dried cranberries
¼ Cup ground almonds
Directions:
In a medium bowl, mix together the nut or seed butter and syrup until smooth and creamy. Stir in the rest of the Ingredients, and mix to make sure the consistency is holding together in a ball. Form the mix into 12 balls.
Place them on a baking sheet lined with parchment or waxed paper and put in the fridge to set for about 15 minutes.
If your balls aren't holding together, it's likely because of the moisture content of your cooked quinoa. Add more nut or seed butter mixed with syrup until it all sticks together.
Nutrition (1 bite) calories: 109; total fat: 7g; carbs: 11g; fiber: 3g; protein: 3g

Almond-Date Energy Bites

Preparation time: 5 minutes • chill time: 15 minutes
Servings: 24 bites
Ingredients
1 cup dates, pitted
1 cup unsweetened shredded coconut
¼ Cup chia seeds
¾ Cup ground almonds
¼ Cup cocoa nibs, or non-dairy chocolate chips
Directions:
Purée everything in a food processor until crumbly and sticking together, pushing down the sides whenever necessary to keep it blending. If you don't have a food processor, you can mash soft medjool dates. But if you're using harder baking dates, you'll have to soak them and then try to purée them in a blender.
Form the mix into 24 balls and place them on a baking sheet lined with parchment or waxed paper. Put in the fridge to set for about 15 minutes. Use the softest dates you can find. Medjool dates are the best for this purpose. The hard dates you see in the baking aisle of your supermarket are going to take a long time to blend up. If you use those, try soaking them in water for at least an hour before you start, and then draining.
Nutrition (1 bite) calories: 152; total fat: 11g; carbs: 13g; fiber: 5g; protein: 3g

Pumpkin pie cups (pressure cooker)

Preparation time: 5 minutes
Serves 4-6
Ingredients
1 cup canned pumpkin purée
1 cup nondairy milk
6 tablespoons unrefined sugar or pure maple syrup (less if using sweetened milk), plus more for sprinkling
¼ Cup spelt flour or all-purpose flour
½ Teaspoon pumpkin pie spice
Pinch salt
Directions
In a medium bowl, stir together the pumpkin, milk, sugar, flour, pumpkin pie spice, and salt. Pour the mixture into 4 heat-proof ramekins. Sprinkle a bit more sugar on the top of each, if you like. Put a trivet in the bottom of your electric pressure cooker's cooking pot and pour in a cup or two of water. Place the ramekins onto the trivet, stacking them if needed (3 on the bottom, 1 on top).
High pressure for 6 minutes. Close and lock the lid, and select high pressure for 6 minutes.
Pressure release. Once the cook time is complete, quick release the pressure. Unlock and remove the lid. Let cool for a few minutes before carefully lifting out the ramekins with oven mitts or tongs. Let cool for at least 10 minutes before serving.
Nutrition calories: 129; total fat: 1g; protein: 3g; sodium: 39mg; fiber: 3g

Coconut and almond truffles

Preparation time: 15 minutes
Cooking time: 0 minutes
Servings: 8 truffles
Ingredients
1 cup pitted dates
1 cup almonds
½ Cup sweetened cocoa powder, plus extra for coating
½ Cup unsweetened shredded coconut
¼ Cup pure maple syrup
1 teaspoon vanilla extract
1 teaspoon almond extract
¼ Teaspoon sea salt
Directions:
In the bowl of a food processor, combine all the **Ingredients** and process until smooth. Chill the mixture for about 1 hour.
Roll the mixture into balls and then roll the balls in cocoa powder to coat.
Serve immediately or keep chilled until ready to serve.

Fudgy Brownies(Pressure cooker)

Preparation time: 10 minutes
Serves 4-6
Ingredients
3 ounces dairy-free dark chocolate
1 tablespoon coconut oil or vegan margarine
½ Cup applesauce
2 tablespoons unrefined sugar
⅓ Cup all-purpose flour
½ Teaspoon baking powder
Pinch salt
Directions
Put a trivet in your electric pressure cooker's cooking pot and pour in a cup or two of two of water. Select sauté or simmer. In a large heat-proof glass or ceramic bowl, combine the chocolate and coconut oil. Place the bowl over the top of your pressure cooker, as you would a double boiler. Stir occasionally until the chocolate is melted, then turn off the pressure cooker. Stir the applesauce and sugar into the chocolate mixture. Add the flour, baking powder, and salt and stir just until combined. Pour the batter into 3 heat-proof ramekins. Put them in a heat-proof dish and cover with aluminum foil. Using a foil sling or silicone helper handles, lower the dish onto the trivet. (alternately, cover each ramekin with foil and place them directly on the trivet, without the dish.)
High pressure for 6 minutes. Close and lock the lid, and select high pressure for 5 minutes.
Pressure release. Once the cook time is complete, quick release the pressure. Unlock and remove the lid.
Let cool for a few minutes before carefully lifting out the dish, or ramekins, with oven mitts or tongs. Let cool for a few minutes more before serving.
Top with fresh raspberries and an extra drizzle of melted chocolate.

Nutrition calories: 316; total fat: 14g; protein: 5g; sodium: 68mg; fiber: 5g

Chocolate macaroons
Preparation time: 10 minutes
Cooking time: 15 minutes
Servings: 8 macaroons
Ingredients
1 cup unsweetened shredded coconut
2 tablespoons cocoa powder
⅔ Cup coconut milk
¼ Cup agave
Pinch of sea salt
Directions:
Preheat the oven to 350°f. Line a baking sheet with parchment paper. In a medium saucepan, cook all the Ingredients over -medium-high heat until a firm dough is formed. Scoop the dough into balls and place on the baking sheet.
Bake for 15 minutes, remove from the oven, and let cool on the baking sheet.
Serve cooled macaroons or store in a tightly sealed container for up to

Chocolate Pudding

Preparation time: 5 minutes
Cooking time: 0 minutes
Servings: 1
Ingredients
1 banana
2 to 4 tablespoons nondairy milk
2 tablespoons unsweetened cocoa powder
2 tablespoons sugar (optional)
½ Ripe avocado or 1 cup silken tofu (optional)
Directions:
In a small blender, combine the banana, milk, cocoa powder, sugar (if using), and avocado (if using). Purée until smooth. Alternatively, in a small bowl, mash the banana very well, and stir in the remaining Ingredients.
Nutrition calories: 244; protein: 4g; total fat: 3g; saturated fat: 1g; carbohydrates: 59g; fiber: 8g

Lime and watermelon granita
Preparation time: 15 minutes • chilling time: 6 hours •
Servings: 4
Ingredients
8 cups seedless -watermelon chunks
Juice of 2 limes, or 2 tablespoons prepared lime juice
½ Cup sugar
Strips of lime zest, for garnish
Directions:
 In a blender or food processor, combine the watermelon, lime juice, and sugar and process until smooth. You may have to do this in two batches. After processing, stir well to combine both batches.

Pour the mixture into a 9-by-13-inch glass dish. Freeze for 2 to 3 hours. Remove from the freezer and use a fork to scrape the top layer of ice. Leave the shaved ice on top and return to the freezer. In another hour, remove from the freezer and repeat. Do this a few more times until all the ice is scraped up. Serve frozen, garnished with strips of lime zest.

Coconut-Banana Pudding

Preparation time: 4 minutes
Cooking time: 5 minutes • overnight to set
Servings: 4
Ingredients
3 bananas, divided
1 (13.5-ounce) can full-fat coconut milk
¼ Cup organic cane sugar
1 tablespoon cornstarch
1 teaspoon vanilla extract
2 pinches sea salt
6 drops natural yellow food coloring (optional)
Ground cinnamon, for garnish
Directions:
 Combine 1 banana, the coconut milk, sugar, cornstarch, vanilla, and
salt in a blender. Blend until smooth and creamy. If you're using the
food coloring, add it to the blender now and blend until the color is
evenly dispersed.
 Transfer to a saucepot and bring to a boil over medium-high heat.
Immediately reduce to a simmer and whisk for 3 minutes, or until
the mixture thickens to a thin pudding and sticks to a spoon.
 Transfer the mixture to a container and allow to cool for 1 hour.
Cover and refrigerate overnight to set. When you're ready to serve,
slice the remaining 2 bananas and build individual servings as
follows: pudding, banana slices, pudding, and so on until a single-
serving dish is filled to the desired level. Sprinkle with ground
cinnamon.

Spiced Apple Chia Pudding

Preparation time: 5 minutes • chill time: 30 minutes
Servings: 1

Ingredients
½ Cup unsweetened applesauce
¼ Cup nondairy milk or canned coconut milk
1 tablespoon chia seeds
1½ teaspoons sugar
Pinch ground cinnamon or pumpkin pie spice

Directions:
In a small bowl, stir together the applesauce, milk, chia seeds, sugar, and cinnamon. Enjoy as is, or let sit for 30 minutes so the chia seeds soften and expand.

Nutrition calories: 153; protein: 3g; total fat: 5g; saturated fat: 1g; carbohydrates: 26g; fiber: 10g

Caramelized pears with balsamic glaze

Preparation time: 5 minutes
Cooking time: 15 minutes
Servings: 4
Ingredients
1 cup balsamic vinegar
¼ Cup plus 3 tablespoons brown sugar
¼ Teaspoon grated nutmeg
Pinch of sea salt
¼ Cup coconut oil
4 pears, cored and cut into slices
Directions:
 In a medium saucepan, heat the balsamic vinegar, ¼ cup of the brown sugar, the nutmeg, and salt over medium-high heat, stirring to thoroughly incorporate the sugar. Allow to simmer, stirring occasionally, until the glaze reduces by half, 10 to 15 minutes.
 Meanwhile, heat the coconut oil in a large sauté pan over medium-high heat until it shimmers. Add the pears to the pan in a single layer. Cook until they turn golden, about 5 minutes. Add the remaining 3 tablespoons brown sugar and continue to cook, stirring occasionally, until the pears caramelize, about 5 minutes more. Place the pears on a plate. Drizzle with balsamic glaze and serve.

Salted Coconut-Almond Fudge

Preparation time: 5 minutes • set time: 1 hour •
Servings: 12
Ingredients
¾ Cup creamy almond butter
½ Cup maple syrup
⅓ Cup coconut oil, softened or melted
6 tablespoons fair-trade unsweetened cocoa powder
1 teaspoon coarse or flaked sea salt
Directions:
 Line a loaf pan with a double layer of plastic wrap. Place one layer horizontally in the pan with a generous amount of overhang, and the second layer vertically with a generous amount of overhang.
 In a medium bowl, gently mix together the almond butter, maple syrup, and coconut oil until well combined and smooth. Add the cocoa powder and gently stir it into the mixture until well combined and creamy.
 Pour the mixture into the prepared pan and sprinkle with the sea salt. Bring the overflowing edges of the plastic wrap over the top of the fudge to completely cover it. Place the pan in the freezer for at least 1 hour or overnight, until the fudge is firm.
Remove the pan from the freezer and lift the fudge out of the pan using the plastic-wrap overhangs to pull it out. Transfer to a cutting board and cut into 1-inch pieces.

Caramelized Bananas

Preparation time: 5 minutes
Cooking time: 10 minutes
Servings: 2
Ingredients
2 tablespoons vegan margarine or coconut oil
2 bananas, peeled, halved crosswise and then lengthwise
2 tablespoons dark brown sugar, demerara sugar, or coconut sugar
2 tablespoons spiced apple cider
Chopped walnuts, for topping

Directions:
 Melt the margarine in a nonstick skillet over medium heat. Add the bananas, and cook for 2 minutes. Flip, and cook for 2 minutes more. Sprinkle the sugar and cider into the oil around the bananas, and cook for 2 to 3 minutes, until the sauce thickens and caramelizes around the bananas. Carefully scoop the bananas into small bowls, and drizzle with any remaining liquid in the skillet. Sprinkle with walnuts.

Nutrition calories: 384; protein: 4g; total fat: 24g; saturated fat: 13g; carbohydrates: 46g; fiber: 5g

Mixed berries and cream

Preparation time: 10 minutes
Cooking time: 0 minutes
Servings: 4
Ingredients
Two 15-ounce cans full-fat coconut milk
3 tablespoons agave
½ Teaspoon vanilla extract
1 pint fresh blueberries
1 pint fresh raspberries
1 pint fresh strawberries, sliced
Directions:
 Refrigerate the coconut milk overnight. When you open the can, the liquid will have separated from the solids. Spoon out the solids and reserve the liquid for another purpose.
 In a medium bowl, whisk the agave and vanilla extract into the coconut solids. Divide the berries among four bowls. Top with the coconut cream. Serve immediately.

Peanut Butter Cups

Preparation time: 20 minutes
Cooking time: 0 minutes
Servings: 12 cups
Ingredients

1½ cups vegan chocolate chips, divided
½ Cup peanut butter, almond or cashew butter, or sunflower seed butter
¼ Cup packed brown sugar
2 tablespoons nondairy milk

Directions:

Line the cups of a muffin tin with paper liners or reusable silicone cups.

In a small microwave-safe bowl, heat ¾ cup of the chocolate chips on high power for 1 minute. Stir. Continue heating in 30-second increments, stirring after each, until the chocolate is melted.

Pour about 1½ teaspoons of melted chocolate into each prepared muffin cup. Set aside, and allow them to harden.

In a small bowl, stir together the peanut butter, brown sugar, and milk until smooth. Scoop about 1½ teaspoons of the mixture on top of the chocolate base in each cup. It's okay if the chocolate is not yet hardened.

Melt the remaining ¾ cup of chocolate chips using the **Directions** in step 1;pour another 1½ teaspoons of chocolate on top of the peanut butter in each cup, softly spreading it to cover. Let the cups sit until the chocolate hardens, about 15 minutes in the refrigerator or several hours on the counter. Leftovers will keep in the refrigerator for up to 2 weeks.

Nutrition (1 cup) calories: 227; protein: 4g; total fat: 14g; saturated fat: 6g; carbohydrates: 22g; fiber: 3g

Spiced rhubarb sauce

Preparation time: 10 minutes
Cooking time: 15 minutes
Servings: 4
Ingredients
½ Cup water
½ Cup sugar
¼ Teaspoon grated nutmeg
¼ Teaspoon ground ginger
¼ Teaspoon ground cinnamon
1 pound rhubarb, cut into ½- to 1-inch pieces
Directions

In a large saucepan, bring the water, sugar, nutmeg, ginger, and cinnamon to a boil. Add the rhubarb and cook over medium-high heat, stirring frequently, until the rhubarb is soft and saucy, about 10 minutes. Chill for at least 30 minutes before serving.

Chocolate-Coconut Bars

Preparation time: 20 minutes • chill time: 20 minutes
Servings: 16 bars
Ingredients
¼ Cup coconut oil or unsalted vegan margarine, plus more for preparing the baking dish (optional)
2 cups unsweetened shredded coconut
¼ Cup sugar
2 tablespoons maple syrup or *simple syrup*
1 cup vegan chocolate chips
Directions:
Coat the bottom and sides of an 8-9 inch-square baking-dish with coconut oil or line it with parchment paper, set aside.
In a bowl, stir the coconut, sugar, maple syrup, and coconut oil. Transfer the mixture to the prepared baking dish, and press it down firmly with the back of a spoon.
Heat the chocolate chips on high power for 1 minute, (in a microwave-safe bowl). Stir. Continue heating in 30-second increments, stir, until the chocolate is melted. Pour the melted chocolate over the coconut base, and let it sit until the chocolate hardens, about 20 minutes. Cut into 16 bars. Keep covered and refrigerated for up to 1 week.
Nutrition (1 bar) calories: 305; protein: 3g; total fat: 26g; saturated fat: 22g; carbohydrates: 19g; fiber: 6g

SAUCES AND DIPS

Cucumber Bites

Preparation time: 10 minutes (excluding soaking time)
Soaking time: 1-3 hours
Servings: 14 bites
Ingredients:
1 cup almonds – soaked 1-3 hours
¼ Cup cashew nuts – soaked 1-3 hours
Juice of 1 lemon
1 clove garlic –minced
Salt & pepper
1 tsp. Olive oil
1 large cucumber – sliced into approximately 1 inch pieces
1 tomato – diced
½ Cup fresh parsley – roughly chopped
Preparation:
Soak almonds and cashew nuts in warm water for 1-3 hours. The longer you soak them, the softer and creamier they will be.
Put all Ingredients (except cucumber, parsley and tomato) into a blender or food processor.
Blend or process until you get a creamy paste.
If the mix is too thick for your likings you can add a little bit of water.
Remove the mixture from the blender.
Add the diced tomato and fresh parsley and gently mix with a spoon.
Scoop one spoonful of mixture onto each cucumber slice.
8. Sprinkle with black pepper and serve.

Broccoli Crispy Bread

Preparation time: 5 minutes
Cooking time: 30 minutes
Servings: 3-4
Ingredients:
4 cups of broccoli florets – cut into chunks
3 tbsp. Nutritional yeast
1 tbsp. Extra virgin olive oil
2 tbsp. Chia seeds
1 tsp. Baking powder
Salt & pepper
½ Cup fresh basil
Preparation:
Preheat oven to 375f.
Soak the chia seeds with 6 tablespoons of water for about 5 minutes.
Put broccoli into a food processor and pulse until you get a texture similar to rice.
Add Nutritional yeast, basil, salt and pepper, and pulse until Ingredients are well combined.
Transfer the mix into a bowl, add olive oil, baking powder, chia seeds and stir well.
Line a baking tray with a sheet of baking paper.
Pour the dough onto the baking paper and spread evenly. The thinner you make it, the crispier it will be.
Bake in the oven for approximately 30 minute until golden and crispy. Make sure it is cooked in the middle.
Remove from the oven and cut into bars.
Enjoy while still warm or cold.

Roasted Pumpkin Seeds

Preparation time: 5 minutes
Cooking time: 25 minutes
Servings: as many as you'd like
Ingredients:
Pumpkin seeds
Extra virgin olive oil
Salt & pepper
Preparation:
Preheat oven to 350f.
Line a baking tray with baking paper or aluminium foil. Either will do.
 Place the seeds into a bowl, drizzle with not too much oil but enough to evenly coat them.
Sprinkle with salt and pepper and toss well together.
Pour the seeds onto the baking tray and roast in the oven for approximately 20 minutes or until they become very lightly brown. Keep an eye on them not to burn them.
During cooking remove the tray a few times to stir the seeds.
When completely roasted, remove from oven and let them cool.
Enjoy as nibbles or sprinkle on your salad or soup.

Multi Seeds Crackers

Preparation time: 10 minutes
Cooking time: 1 hour
Servings: 20-30 crackers (depending on your cuts)
Ingredients:
½ Cup chia seeds
½ Cup sunflower seeds
½ Cup pumpkin seeds
½ Cup sesame seeds
1 cup water
1 large clove garlic or 2 small – minced
Salt & pepper

Preparation:
Preheat oven to 300f.
Put all seeds into a large bowl and add water. Stir well until combined.
Let the seeds rest for 3-5 minutes until the chia seeds absorb the water.
Stir again. There should be no more water on the bottom of the bowl.
Use a spatula to spread the mixture onto the baking paper. Spread into two rectangles approximately 12"x 7" in size and approximately 1/8 to ¼ inch thick.
Sprinkle with salt and pepper.
Bake in the oven for 35 minutes.
Remove from oven and turn the rectangles around very carefully with a spatula.
Put back in the oven and back for another 25-35 minutes.
Keep an eye on them to make sure they don't burn.
Remove from oven when the edges are lightly golden.

Set aside to cool down for approximately 10 minutes.
Break the rectangles into crackers and let to cool completely.
You can store these crackers in an airtight container for up to 1
month, but we honestly think they will not last you that long as they
are too moreish!

Almond Cauliflower

Preparation time: 5 minutes
Cooking time: 30 minutes
Servings: 4

Ingredients:
4 cups cauliflower florets – chopped into bite size chunks
1 tbsp. Extra virgin olive oil
2 tbsp. Almonds – chopped in very small pieces

Preparation:
Preheat oven to 425f.
Line a baking tray with baking paper.
Place cauliflower into a bowl, add olive oil, salt and pepper, almonds and toss everything well together.
Pour the cauliflower onto the baking paper.
Bake in oven for approximately 30 minutes or until golden brown and soft. Stir occasionally.
Remove from oven, sprinkle with ground black pepper and serve.

Tahini Dressing

Preparation time: 5 minutes
Servings: 4-5

Ingredients:
¼ Cup tahini paste
Juice of 1 lemon
1 tbsp. Apple cider vinegar
2 tbsp. Extra virgin olive oil
2 clove of garlic – minced
Salt & pepper

Preparation:
Place all Ingredients into a blender (except for water).
Blend until creamy.
If the dressing is too thick, add a little bit of water until it reaches
    the desired consistency.

Lemon & Mustard Vinaigrette

Preparation time: 5 minutes
Servings: 6 tablespoons
Ingredients:
Juice of 1 lemon
½ Tsp. Dijon mustard
4 tbsp. Extra virgin olive oil
Salt & pepper
Preparation:
Put lemon juice, mustard, salt and pepper into a bowl.
Whisk well until combined.
While whisking, drizzle in the extra virgin olive oil.
Keep whisking vigorously until all Ingredients are combined and you have a medium creamy dressing.
The dressing should be ready at this point. You can taste and adjust any of the Ingredients to taste.

Cheesy Sauce

Preparation time: 5 minutes
Servings: 4
Ingredients:
2 tbsp. Extra virgin olive oil
2 tbsp. Nutritional yeast
Juice of 1 lemon
Salt & pepper
Preparation:
Combine all Ingredients together into a bowl and whisk vigorously.
Serve as an accompaniment to your dishes.

Chimichurri Style Sauce

Preparation time: 1-2 minutes
Cooking time: 5 minutes
Servings: 2/3 cup
Ingredients:
½ Cup extra virgin olive oil
1 tsp. Fresh rosemary
1 tsp. Fresh oregano
2 medium cloves garlic – crushed
2 tsp. Smoked paprika
1 bay leaf
¼ Tsp. Sea salt
1 tbsp. Lemon juice
Pinch of black pepper flakes
Preparation:
Put the herbs into a mortar and pestle and lightly pound them. If you do not have a mortar and pestle you can chop them very finely.
Pour olive oil into a pan and warm over medium-low heat.
When oil is hot, remove from heat.
Stir paprika, black pepper flakes, bay leaf and a pinch of salt into the oil.
Add herbs and lemon juice.
Put the sauce into a jar in the fridge and leave it to infuse for a couple of days before using.

Peanut Sauce

Preparation time: 10 minutes
Cooking time: 5 minutes
Servings: 1 cup
Ingredients:
½ Cup creamy peanut butter
2 tbsp. Thai red curry paste
¾ Cup coconut milk
2tbsp. Apple cider vinegar
1/2 tbsp. Coconut palm sugar
2 tbsp. Ground peanuts

Salt

Preparation:
Add all Ingredients together into a saucepan and whisk well.
Transfer the pan to the stove and heat up the mix over a low heat while continuing whisking.
Keep a constant eye on the sauce and as soon as it starts bubbling remove from heat. If you like the sauce more liquid, add a little bit of water and whisk. Keep adding water bit by bit until it reaches your desired consistency.
Move the sauce into a bowl and top with ground peanuts.

Spicy Almond & Garlic Dip

Preparation time: 5 minutes
Soaking time: overnight
Servings: 1 large cup
Ingredients:
1 cup raw almonds
1 cup almond milk
2 cloves garlic
½ Tsp. Chili powder
¼ Tsp. Smoked paprika
Pinch of salt
Pinch of cayenne pepper
Preparation:
Soak almonds overnight.
Put all Ingredients into a blender.
Blend until smooth and creamy.
You can use immediately or refrigerate covered.

Cauliflower Hummus

Preparation time: 5 minutes
Cooking time: 5 minutes
Servings: 2 cups
Ingredients:
4 cups cauliflower stems and florets – chopped
2 tbsp. Tahini paste
5 tbsp. Extra virgin olive oil
Juice of 2 lemons
Salt & pepper
Pinch of cumin
Preparation:
Steam or lightly boil cauliflower for approximately 5 minutes or until soft.
Drain and let it cool down completely.
Combine cauliflower, tahini paste, extra virgin olive oil, lemon juice and cumin into a food processor. Process until creamy.
Alternatively, you can use a blender.
Add salt and pepper to taste.
You might want to taste it and add more lemon juice or olive oil according to taste.
Serve with raw vegetables.

Eggplant & Walnut Spread

Preparation time: 10-15 minutes
Cooking time: 45 minutes
Servings: 1 large cup

Ingredients:
2 x medium round eggplants
1 tbsp. Extra virgin olive oil
1 cup walnuts – chopped
2 cloves garlic
Juice of 1 large lemon
Salt & pepper
1 tsp. Cumin
1/3 cup tahini paste
½ Cup fresh parsley leaves

Preparation:
Preheat oven to 375f.
Place eggplants on a baking tray and rub them with the olive oil.
Stab them with a knife a couple times.
Roast for 45 minutes until they look deflated and wrinkled.
In the meantime, toast the walnuts in a pan over medium-high heat for 3-4 minutes. Leave to cool.
When eggplant is cooked, remove from oven and let it cool down.
Cut the eggplants in half and scoop the flesh out into a food processor.
Add walnuts and all other Ingredients. Process until obtaining a paste.
Serve into a bowl with a drizzle of extra virgin olive oil accompanied by crackers or raw vegetables.

Coconut Yogurt Dip

Preparation time: 10 minutes
Servings: 2 cups

Ingredients:
1 ½ cup coconut yogurt
1 large cucumber – peeled and cut into chunks
3 cloves garlic
Juice of 1 lemon
2 tbsp. Extra virgin olive oil
½ Cup fresh coriander – finely chopped
Salt & pepper

Preparation:
Place all Ingredients (except coriander) into a blender and blend until smooth.
Add salt and pepper to taste and the coriander.
Mix well with a spoon.
Refrigerate for about 1 hour to let the flavors infuse.
Stir the dip well before serving.

Olive Tapenade

Preparation time: 5 minutes
Servings: 1 cup

Ingredients:
½ Cup black olives
½ Cup green olives
2 cloves garlic
1tsp. Lemon juice
Ground black pepper

Preparation:
Put all Ingredients together into a food processor and process for few seconds. You basically want all Ingredients finely chopped and well mixed together. Be careful not processes for too long otherwise you will have a paste.
Serve to spread onto your favorite crackers.

Chunky Rocket Spread

Preparation time: 15 minutes
Servings: 1 cup

Ingredients:
1 ½ cup roasted cashew nuts
1 clove garlic
3 cups rocket leaves
¼ Cup Nutritional yeast
¼ Cup extra virgin olive oil
Juice of ½ lemon
Salt & pepper

Preparation:
Place the cashew nuts, garlic and Nutritional yeast into a food processor.
Pulse gently until the nuts are still chunky and mixed well together with the other Ingredients.
Transfer the mix into a bowl.
Place olive oil and lemon juice into the food processor, then add rocket leaves and pulse to blend.
Transfer the rocket mixture into the bowl with the cashews, season with salt and pepper and mix together with a spoon.
Serve with crackers or other low carb breads.

CONCLUSION

There you have it. You are now well on your way to weight the Vegan way!

Be prepared to feel great, have energy you never had before and achieve the weight loss results you always desired! Thank you for taking the time to read my book and stay tuned for more books on Veganism in the future.

Thanks again for your support!

Lightning Source UK Ltd.
Milton Keynes UK
UKHW020114140123
415288UK00011B/141